Look at Me!

by Willa Reid

illustrated by Amy Vangsgard

⭐ Strategy Focus

As we read this story, let's think about all the things the girl puts on.

 HOUGHTON MIFFLIN   BOSTON

Look at my socks.

Look at my boots.

Look at my sweater.

Look at my coat.

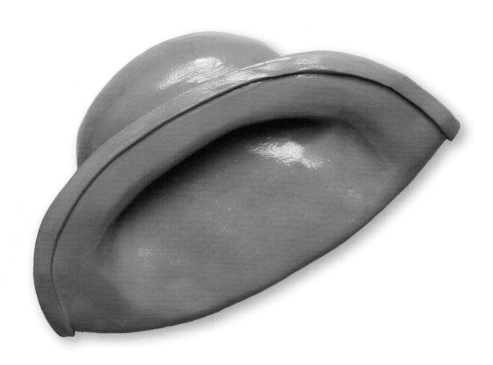

Look at my hat.

Look at my umbrella.

Look at me!